VINTAGE JOHN DEERE

Text and photographs by Dave Arnold

Voyageur Press

Edited by Andrea Rud and Helene Anderson
Designed by Andrea Rud and Lou Gordon
Cover designed by Andrea Rud
Printed in China
95 96 97 98 99   5 4 3 2 1

Library of Congress Cataloging-in-Publication Data
Arnold, Dave, 1942–
        Vintage John Deere / text and photographs by Dave Arnold.
               p.   cm.
        Includes index.
        ISBN 0-89658-265-5
        1. John Deere tractors—Collectors and collecting. 2. John Deere tractors—
History. I. Title
        TL233.5.A74   1995
        629.225—dc20 94-31815
               CIP

Please write or call, or stop by, for our free catalog of publications. Our toll-free number to place an order or to obtain a free catalog is 800-888-9653.

Educators, fundraisers, premium and gift buyers, publicists, and marketing managers: Looking for creative products and new sales ideas? Voyageur Press books are available at special discounts when purchased in quantities, and special editions can be created to your specifications. For details contact our marketing department.

Page 1: Production of the 730 diesel unit began in 1958 and ended in 1960 with Deere's corporate-wide move away from the two-cylinder engine. **Page 3:** A fine restored example of the Waterloo Boy Model N from the Bellin collection. **Page 4:** John Deere tractors have always been pleasant to the eye, but orchard models, such as this 1952 AO with its "swoopy" sheet metal, have a particular attraction. **Page 5:** A 1939 John Deere BWH40 designed for vegetable farming tasks.

Published by Voyageur Press, Inc.
P.O. Box 338, 123 North Second Street
Stillwater, MN 55082 U.S.A.
612-430-2210, fax 612-430-2211

Distributed in Canada by
Raincoast Books
8680 Cambie Street
Vancouver, B.C. V6P 6M9

Distributed in Europe by
Midland Publishing Ltd.
24 The Hollow, Earl Shilton
Leicester LE9 7NA, England
Tel 01455 233747

ACKNOWLEDGMENTS

My sincere appreciation is expressed to Mike Bellin, who made
equipment available to photograph, provided advice on the finer points
of specific units, and answered questions whenever asked.

DEDICATION

To AlexAnn Nadine Koecher, a new arrival as this book goes to press.
May your future be based on the good from the past
and your contributions help create the best of what is to come.

CONTENTS

JOHN DEERE: TRANSFORMING THE AMERICAN FARM

It was the middle 1800s, and for one group of hardy American adventurers the great westward migration, which had begun at the turn of the decade, had come to a grinding halt. Crop farmers in search of the widely heralded new lands upon which to build homesteads, plant crops, and raise families found themselves facing an unanticipated problem. As these settlers approached the American prairie and began to enter the Mississippi River valley watershed, they encountered a soil type unknown in the farming lands of their heritage. Here the soil, in contrast to played-out eastern and European land, was virgin, rich, and full of potential for outstanding crops. It also was sticky, and therein lay the reason for the halt in the travelers' westward progress. The standard plow of the time was constructed of a cast iron share and a wooden moldboard. Adequate for eastern farms, it quickly became bogged down in the prairie soils of the Midwest. These sticky soils tended to compact into clods and adhere to plow surfaces, causing greatly increased drag and erratic travel through the soil. The only solution seemed to be to stop, scrape the plow clean, drop it back into the now-

ragged furrow, and start again—only to have the problem recur within precious few feet. Draft animals suffered, plows and hitching lines were over-stressed, and a farmer's patience quickly wore thin.

It was during this period that a Vermont blacksmith, eager to find a town on the newly emerging western frontier in which to establish his business, arrived in a place called Grand Detour in the state of Illinois. So named by the French because the Rock River made a 180-degree "grand detour" and headed due north before again resuming its southerly course, this territory was a part of the Mississippi valley watershed and thus an area with the problematic, sticky soils.

Setting up shop in Grand Detour, the Vermonter John Deere began performing the usual tasks expected of a blacksmith. In the course of his activities, he became aware of the local farmers' difficulties in tilling the soil. Out of natural curiosity, and with encouragement from locals, he looked into the problem. At first Deere turned his efforts to the then-current plow, attempting to modify or refine the design. Initial efforts proved fruitless. It was not until a chance

A threshing show.

encounter with the gleaming polished surface of a broken sawmill blade that Deere began to visualize a solution to the problem. A quickly made prototype proved successful and resulted in orders from farmers for similar units. John Deere had adopted a high-grade steel with good polishing characteristics to the common plow and developed the first self-scouring plow capable of turning American prairie soils. The westward move of the American crop farmers resumed, riding on the polished, self-scouring plow developed and manufactured at the John Deere Plow Works.

According to government statistics, in the 1840s eighty-four out of every one hundred Americans lived and worked in rural areas. A high percentage of these eighty-four worked the land or were engaged in an agricultural pursuit in some form or another. Farming was both big business and a way of life for most Americans. To put this into perspective, we should realize that by the 1840s the steam engine was already 150 years old. Descendants of Robert Fulton's original steamship routinely propelled themselves up rivers and across the Great Lakes. Great cities such as Chicago, New York, and Baltimore boasted significant manufacturing sectors powered by the latest in steam-manufacturing equipment. America was at the forefront of the Industrial Revolution. Progress was on a roll—every place, it seemed, except down on the farm.

While mechanical innovation was rampant in America's manufacturing centers, the American farmer struggled with equipment and methods substantially unchanged from the days of Christ. The typical farm family moving west in 1840 possessed a breaking plow, a stubble plow (now ineffectual in the prairie soil), a harrow, a single-shovel plow to cultivate corn, and a miscellaneous collection of hand tools such as hoes, rakes, pitch forks, and scythes. It was into this environment that John Deere stepped in 1837 with his highly polished self-scouring plow—an environment badly in need of the creativity and innovation which characterized most other segments of American society during this period.

A factory experimental B unit or an aftermarket modification? Nobody knows for sure.

IN THE BEGINNING

Pages 10–11: Animal power and very limited mechanical innovation characterized the American farming picture into which John Deere stepped in 1837 with his self-scouring plow. Here we see an example of the animal and human requirements necessary to thresh a crop in the late 1800s. Ten sturdy work horses and three to five men constitute only the "power plant" portion of this threshing crew—other men were needed to operate the separator, seen at left. It's easy to see the appeal of the steam and subsequent gas tractors that organizations such as Deere & Company would produce by the tens of thousands in the years to follow. Note also the horse-drawn Deering reaper in the small photo.

 Right: Pictured is the steel-beam, single-furrow, self-scouring walking plow of the type produced by Deere from 1867 into the 1940s. The self-scouring plow was the start of a green and yellow dynasty that grew to encompass the world. Blacksmith John Deere's use of highly polished, high-quality steel taken from a damaged lumber mill saw blade solved the problem of sticking soils encountered by crop farmers new to the Mississippi River watershed. Not only did this new design scour itself, but continual use resulted in an even more highly polished surface. It is interesting to note in this day of conservation tillage and no-till planting that this single product, on which the Deere empire was founded, is slowly falling out of favor. Shown here is an example of a standard unit for use with horses. This unit sold by the tens of thousands. **Below:** A standard tractor-drawn, single-bottom plow of the type built by the thousands by Deere.

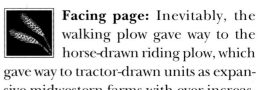

Facing page: Inevitably, the walking plow gave way to the horse-drawn riding plow, which gave way to tractor-drawn units as expansive midwestern farms with ever-increasing acreage were opened for cultivation. By the early 1850s, Deere had begun a diversification process that would create a wide range of tillage and planting implements and, eventually, tractors— the much-needed source of power for this expanding line of products. Noted here is an early horse-drawn, single-bottom "sulky" or riding plow. **Insets:** More examples of John Deere horse-drawn, three-wheeled sulky plows.

15

 Facing page: A John Deere two-bottom unit with the moldboard portion of one plow totally worn out, no doubt due to years of endless tillage work. The lower portion of the plow (note the horizontal seam running in line with the bottom edge of the moldboard damage) is called the share and is the part of the plow that actually cuts the soil, while the moldboard, or the upper portion, turns the soil over. **This page:** A horse-drawn, ground-wheel-driven Deere corn binder, circa 1915. This is an early form of harvesting equipment that cut and tied corn stalks into bundles and dropped them in the field for later collection.

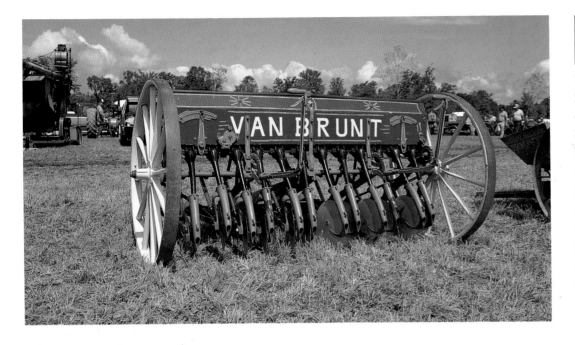

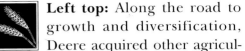 **Left top:** Along the road to growth and diversification, Deere acquired other agricultural manufacturers. Foremost in the field of seeders was the Van Brunt organization, founded in 1860 in Mayville, Wisconsin. Deere purchased Van Brunt in 1911 and continued to use the name for years afterward. **Left bottom:** With the advent of large and powerful steam traction engines, it was only natural that the world's most successful plow manufacturer would produce large gangs of plows to be pulled by these huge engines. Here we see one such unit, typical of those manufactured from the 1910s through the 1930s, in a prairie setting reminiscent of the territory in which it was used. **Facing page:** In 1908 Deere entered into an agreement to have the Marseilles Manufacturing Co. of Marseilles, Illinois, produce corn shellers to be sold under the Deere & Mansur trade name. This relationship prospered, and in 1910 Deere purchased Marseilles and added corn shellers to its product offerings.

Pages 20–22: The year 1912 was pivotal in John Deere history. At that time the company's board of directors began the investigation of a "tractor plow," a self-propelled unit capable of pulling a single plow. With its by-now wide array of drawn tillage products, it was evident to forward thinkers at Deere that, if nothing else, a modern power unit capable of pulling the company's products would help sell more of the already developed product line. Researchers conducted experiments, tested prototypes, examined competitive products, and undertook a multitude of other efforts. This all culminated in Deere & Company's March 1918 purchase of the Waterloo Gasoline Engine Company, by then a very successful manufacturer of stationary engines and tractors. Primary among the units produced by Waterloo Company were the R and N model tractors, dubbed Waterloo Boys. The R was produced from 1916 through 1919 and included a production run of just over eight thousand units. The N model followed the R and was produced through 1924, totaling about twenty thousand units. Both tractors were powered by a nearly identical horizontal, in-line, two-cylinder engine advertised by the factory at twelve drawbar horsepower and twenty-five belt horsepower. The R model had one speed for forward and one speed for reverse, while the N model carried two forward speeds and one reverse. Shown here are a stationary engine (**top inset**) and restored examples of the Model N.

During this period, manufacturers' horsepower ratings for both stationary engines and tractors were, at best, often inaccurate. It was not unheard of for a manufacturer to simply change a paint

21

color and suddenly acquire a few more horsepower to keep step with the competition. An empirical test or set of standards was needed to provide meaningful data for the consumer. Out of this need was born the Nebraska Tractor Tests, a set of standards against which all farm tractors could be tested and rated. It's interesting to note that the very first test in this now-famous series was conducted in April of 1920 on a Model N Waterloo Boy. It was found to produce just over 25 belt horsepower and 15.98 drawbar horsepower.

Note the relatively lower height of the fuel (kerosene) tank on the above unit, indicative of early Model N units.

 Note the general engine design and layout on this Waterloo Boy owned by the Bellin family of Isanti, Minnesota. This was an indicator of things to come from the John Deere line for the next forty years. Push rods, rocker arms, and valve stems were exposed to dust and dirt. Lubrication was strictly manual and had to be performed on a hourly basis when the machine was at work in the fields.

DEERE'S
OWN TRACTORS

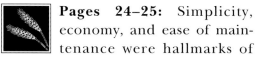 **Pages 24–25:** Simplicity, economy, and ease of maintenance were hallmarks of Deere's new Model D, released to the market in March 1923. The by-then characteristic two-cylinder engine carried a bore and stroke of six and one-half inches by seven inches and, according to Nebraska Tractor Test number 102 dated April 1924, produced 30.4 belt horsepower and 22.53 drawbar horsepower. By July 1935, as recorded in Nebraska Tractor Test number 236, the Model D, with a slightly larger engine, produced 41.59 belt horsepower and 30.74 drawbar horsepower. At the cessation of production in 1953, horsepower was up to 42 at the belt pulley and 38 at the drawbar.

Shown here is an early "unstyled" Model D in the mud at a Midwest threshing show **(small photo)** and a later, "styled" D at rest during the annual Rollag spectacle **(large photo).** To John Deere enthusiasts, "unstyled" describes tractors that, depending on specific models, were manufactured before 1939.

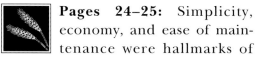 **Above:** The very earliest models utilized a twenty-six-inch spoked flywheel, carried a two–forward-speed transmission, and rode on a fabricated front axle based on a trusslike arrangement of welded steel rods. This front axle was quickly dropped in favor of a cast beam axle, and the spoked flywheel evolved to a twenty-four-inch spoked unit that, by 1926, became a one-piece cast wheel splined to the crankshaft. In all, the Model D was in continuous production, in both unstyled and styled versions, from 1923 through 1953, resulting in approximately 162,000 units placed in the field. The spoked unit pictured here is a 1924 Model D with a twenty-four-inch flywheel and standard factory rear wheel lugs. It is just one of many John Deere units in the Mike Bellin collection in Isanti, Minnesota.

 Below: Competition in the marketplace, this time in the form of the International Harvester Farmall—a superb cultivating tractor of the period—forced competitors to consider production of a lightweight, versatile, general-purpose unit. Deere's answer was the General Purpose (GP) tractor designed for a variety of tasks and modified at the factory for a number of specialized applications. Here we see a handful of stern-faced enthusiasts crowded around a 1928 GP owned by Lynn Erickson from Mora, Minnesota. The tractor is driving a dynamometer at the annual White Pines Threshing Show in McGrath, Minnesota.

Above: In the late 1930s, pushed by competition and a desire to further differentiate its line in the marketplace, John Deere embarked on a program that would clean up the company's image and give Deere equipment a newer, more modern appearance. Deere & Company contracted the New York firm of Henry Dreyfuss Associates, an industrial design organization. The results were first seen in 1939 with the styled A and B models and then with the styled D and L models. Noted here are examples of styled Ds much as they appeared in the 1940s, without the chrome exhaust, of course, on the 1944 unit.

 Introduced as a full production run in 1937, Deere's smallest tractor was considered by the factory to fall under the General Purpose umbrella. Powered by a two-cylinder engine, these units were built for cultivating, towing, and single-plow use. The earliest models were designated Model 62. By 1938 this unit carried the Model L designation, and in 1939 the success-ful styling efforts, so evident on the larger tractors, were applied to the Model L, as exemplified by the unit with the umbrella **(above).** Also shown is Mike Bellin's 1938 unstyled L **(left).** In 1940 power was increased from 9 to 13.1 drawbar horsepower, and the unit was redesigned as the Model LA. The L series introduced to the tractor world the concept of offset engine and driver

positions. Incorporated partly due to necessity—if the operator sat directly behind the engine the tractor would have had to be lengthened—and partly for better visibility, this feature aided cultivation significantly. **Facing page:** An early, unstyled Model L at rest after moving a hay press into position for the task at hand.

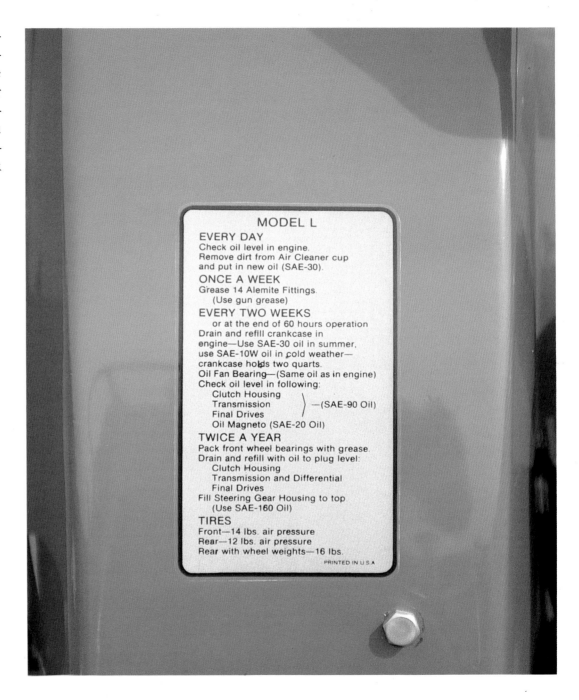

MODEL L

EVERY DAY
Check oil level in engine.
Remove dirt from Air Cleaner cup
and put in new oil (SAE-30).

ONCE A WEEK
Grease 14 Alemite Fittings.
    (Use gun grease)

EVERY TWO WEEKS
    or at the end of 60 hours operation
Drain and refill crankcase in
engine—Use SAE-30 oil in summer,
use SAE-10W oil in cold weather—
crankcase holds two quarts.
Oil Fan Bearing—(Same oil as in engine)
Check oil level in following:
    Clutch Housing
    Transmission   —(SAE-90 Oil)
    Final Drives
    Oil Magneto (SAE-20 Oil)

TWICE A YEAR
Pack front wheel bearings with grease.
Drain and refill with oil to plug level:
    Clutch Housing
    Transmission and Differential
    Final Drives
Fill Steering Gear Housing to top.
    (Use SAE-160 Oil)

TIRES
Front—14 lbs. air pressure
Rear—12 lbs. air pressure
Rear with wheel weights—16 lbs.

PRINTED IN U.S.A.

The year 1934 marked the start of a revolution at John Deere. The Model D, the company's successful early heavyweight, was still a good seller, and the recently introduced General Purpose tractor was a hit, but the competition, not to mention the dreary Depression economy, were having a serious impact on John Deere sales. The International Farmall, with its low price, overall versatility, and excellent cultivating qualities, pointed the way to

the future. Small- to medium-size farms didn't need the heavyweight features of the Model D and, in addition, the D wasn't a cultivator. If you owned a Model D, you likely still maintained horses for cultivating row crops. The GP was a start toward a lighter, more versatile tractor, but it wasn't serious competition for the Farmall. The writing was on the wall. Versatility, low cost, and row crop capability were features that would sell in the marketplace. Deere's answer was the

Model A **(above),** advertised as a replacement for six horses. Introduced in 1934, it would become the single most popular tractor in the Deere line, remaining in production through 1952. It was capable of pulling two plows, its rear wheel width was adjustable from fifty-six inches to eighty-four inches, it incorporated a power take-off (PTO), and it was the first unit to introduce the hydraulic lifting and control of drawn implements.

With the introduction of the A came a lot of different looks and possibilities, depending on a farmer's needs. Front ends as well as rear wheels could be set narrow or wide. New specialty models entered the line. While steel wheels remained a factory option (a few actually being sold each year all the way through 1960), rubber became an alternative in 1930. Shown here **(left)** is the green spline on the axle shaft of either an A or B, which allowed rear wheel width adjustments. **Right top and facing page:** Note also the differing steel cleats on the two As shown here. The unit pulling the haying equipment (**facing page**) has the factory option "skeleton steel" wheels, with the reversed spikes to minimize soil penetration and increase flotation. The A, with four steel wheels (**right top**), carries the more frequently seen standard four-inch spade lugs. **Right bottom:** Here we get a closer look at steel wheels with standard four-inch spade lugs.

⑤ **YOU CAN SIT OR STAND AT WILL**

The John Deere Model A is provided with both seat and foot platform. This is a decided advantage. By standing, the operator can relieve fatigue, get above the dust in extreme conditions or get a better view of the work, in extremely bad condition.

⑥ **CENTERED HITCH ELIMINATES SIDE DRAFT IN PLOWING**

By setting the wheels in on the axles to 56" tread, you get practically a centered hitch on both plow and tractor which largely overcomes side draft.

No extra effort is required in guiding the tractor when plowing and the quality work of the plow is not affected.

⑦ **LIGHT WEIGHT—WELL BALANCED**

This new John Deere General Purpose weighs only 3525 lbs. Compare this with similar-powered tractors. You will quickly recognize this as another reason why this tractor is more economical. A definite penalty is attached to excess weight in increased fuel consumption which is eliminated in this new tractor.

⑧ **FOUR SPEEDS FORWARD**

The operator has 4 forward speeds with which to meet conditions on various jobs. Speeds of 2⅓ and 3⅓ M.P.H. are provided for the heavier jobs such as plowing, disking, bedding, planting, harvesting, corn picking, etc. The higher speeds of 4¾ and 6¾ M.P.H. are available and suitable for lighter draw-bar work and for speedy transportation to and from the fields. Equipped with low-pressure pneumatic tires the 6¾ M.P.H. speed permits the owner to use his tractor effectively on the road for hauling or transporting. The four speeds built into this new tractor materially widen its field of utility.

⑨ **SIMPLE—EASILY ACCESSIBLE**

The John Deere Model A can be serviced from a standing position. Under no conditions does it become necessary to crawl under the tractor or lie on your back to get at parts.

Because the valves and valve seats are located in the cylinder head it is an easy job to service this part of the tractor yourself on the farm. On John Deere Tractors servicing costs are extremely low because the average operator can do all the work himself and save the cost of hiring a mechanic.

- 4 -

JOHN DEERE MODEL A GENERAL PURPOSE TRACTOR WITH ADJUSTABLE TREAD
(Fly-wheel-Side View)

—AND, IN ADDITION, THE JOHN DEERE MODEL A IS BUILT FOR MORE YEARS OF BETTER SERVICE

VALVE-IN-HEAD TYPE ENGINE   A valve-in-head engine is built into the John Deere Model A because this type has the following advantages:

—greater fuel economy.

—better torque or hanging-on ability under peak loads, resulting from a more compact combustion-chamber which permits a more rapid intake of fuel, better and more complete burning of the fuel and a more rapid expulsion of burned gases.

—easier to service because valves and seats are located in the cylinder head which makes valve grinding and replacement of parts a simple and inexpensive job.

—increased durability because of the location of the valves in the cylinder head.

This is the same type of engine that has been used so successfully in the famous John Deere Model D Tractor.

- 5 -

A sales brochure for Model A tractors with adjustable treads. Highlighted features include "both a seat and a foot platform," "a centered hitch," and "four speeds forward."

 As efficient and versatile as the Model A was, the market still needed a unit smaller than the A to be used on the many small farms for which animal power could still be economically justified. The year 1935 saw John Deere's introduction of the Model B. The B was designed as a one-plow tractor and was advertised to replace four horses on a typical farm. This new tractor weighed approximately nine hundred pounds less than the A, and carried the same features as its bigger brother. Power was rated at 9 at the drawbar and 14 at the pulley. As with the Model A, the Model B sprouted a number of variations to suit specific farming needs. The photos here show two B standards, both on steel, one **(left bottom)** with standard four-inch spade lugs and the other **(left top)** mounted on "skeleton steel" rear wheels, designed for use in heavy clay or gumbo soils. This design offered less surface area to which these soils could cling, thereby minimizing the opportunity for buildup and loss of traction.

Facing page: A BN (Model B, Narrow) with its single pneumatic front tire. **Top inset:** A BW (Model B, Wide) with its adjustable front axle. **Center inset:** Shown here is a later model, a styled B rigged for the task for which it was superbly qualified. Lightweight and nimble, the B was the ideal tractor for cultivation tasks. **Bottom inset:** The rear portion of a Deere cultivating rig.

STYLED TRACTORS

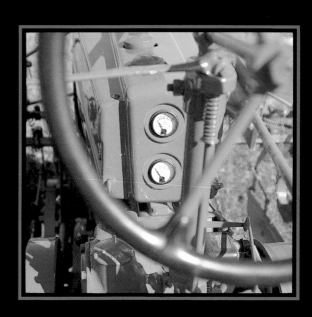

Pages 40–41: By 1939 John Deere was looking seriously into stylizing its line in order to compete with other manufacturers who were beginning such efforts. The goal was to better differentiate its tractors from competitive units and give the line a more modern look, as exemplified by the automobile manufacturers of the period. The results of that effort were successful, to say the least. Dreyfuss Associates gave the line a smooth, strong, forceful appearance. From the now-popular A and B models through the old D model, all emerged with bold and streamlined features. Just as the automobile had lost its square shape and angular lines of the late twenties and thirties in favor of the sculptured, flowing look of the forties, so too had Deere replaced the squared, bolted-together look in favor of streamlined horizontal and vertical lines. A new look and new presence was achieved, one that would last virtually unchanged for twenty years.

Shown in the large photo is a standard two-front-wheel tricycle Model A. Note the strong horizontal lines in the radiator grill and the hood, similar to those found on highway and high performance race cars of the thirties and forties. In the small photo, we see the driver's view.

A sales brochure for Model A and B tractors. Page 2 of the brochure shows a Model B, and page 3 features a Model A.

Left top: Noted here is a somewhat uncommon AN (Model A, Narrow), with its standard pressed steel frame. **Left bottom:** In contrast to the above AN, this photo displays the styled appearance of an AW (Model A, Wide).

Even the sixteen-year-old D model was restyled in 1939 and given a major facelift. The new design spawned a very forceful, bulldog appearance, indicative of its senior place in the Deere line and its strengths in the field. By 1936 the marketing corps at Deere was back to its usual cry for more power, more versatility. The A was a success but it was limited to two plows, and in the wrong soils its performance was sometimes marginal. Versatility was great, however. What the marketing people wanted was a bigger machine, a tractor with the same features and versatility of the A but with three plow capacity. From this need was born the Model G in 1937. Unstyled at its introduction, it received the Dreyfuss treatment in 1941 along with a six-speed transmission replacing the original four-speed gearbox. At the time of introduction the G was the largest row crop tractor on the market.

Here we see a GN (Model G, Narrow front) **(right top),** and a GW (Wide front) **(right bottom).** The Model G was manufactured with the usual horizontal, inline, two-cylinder engine with a 6 1/8-inch bore and a seven-inch stroke designed to operate at a governed speed of 975 RPM. It produced 20.7 horsepower at the drawbar and 31.4 horsepower at the belt pulley. Production ran from 1937 (see advertising brochure, opposite) to 1953.

A Heavy-Duty General Purpose Tractor of Comparatively Light Weight

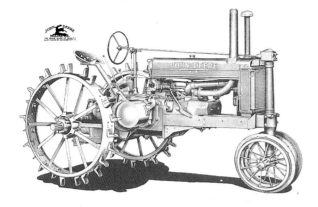

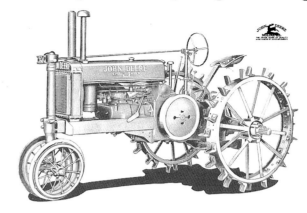

Simple — Dependable — Long-Lived

The outstanding advantage of the John Deere Model "G" Tractor is its powerful, smooth-running, two-cylinder engine, making possible the utmost simplicity and a minimum of parts to require adjustment and eventual replacement.

Fewer and heavier parts last longer, give the tractor longer life. Maintenance cost is lower, and you can make the majority of required adjustments yourself.

Because of the exclusive design of the two-cylinder engine, the Model "G" burns low-cost fuels successfully, just as have all other John Deere Tractors over a period of many years. This is a material saving. The power of the engine is delivered directly to the drive wheels through spur gears, without bevel gears which consume power. On belt work every ounce of engine power is delivered to the pulley which is mounted right on the crankshaft.

The life of the engine is guarded by a full-pressure force-feed lubricating system with oil-filter, oil wash-down air cleaner, crankcase breather and ventilator, fuel filter and a complete enclosure of all working parts. The Model "G" will give long-time satisfaction.

A Pleasure to Operate

You will find the Model "G" Tractor easy to operate. The two-cylinder, valve-in-head engine has plenty of power, plenty of ability to "hang on" under sustained loads, and it operates with the utmost smoothness. Care in weighing and balancing pistons and connecting rods, care in balancing the rugged crankshaft, flywheel, and belt pulley assembly, statically as well as dynamically, with control exercised by the sensitive governor, assures smooth flowing power. It is really a pleasure to operate the John Deere Model "G" General Purpose Tractor.

Extra-Value Features

There are many extra-value features built into the John Deere Model "G" Tractor. There are heavier parts, stronger parts all the way through. A new, manually controlled radiator shutter, with guard, can be operated from the tractor platform. The operator can easily maintain accurate engine temperature, on cold days or hot, going with the wind or against it, which means more uniform engine performance and an even greater measure of operating economy.

Foot-controlled differential brakes, ample clearance under the axles, 60- to 84-inch adjustment of rear wheel tread, convenient hitch which is fully adjustable vertically and horizontally and which remains permanently on the tractor, built-in power shaft, and the most modern hydraulic power lift . . . these are all features which save labor, cut your farming costs, and speed up your work.

Four-Speed Transmission

To obtain any one of four forward speeds, or reverse, simply operate the single gear shift lever. Speeds, when tractor is equipped with $51\frac{1}{2}$-inch steel wheels, are: (1st) $2\frac{1}{4}$ m.p.h., (2nd) $3\frac{1}{4}$ m.p.h., (3rd) $4\frac{1}{4}$ m.p.h., (4th) 6 m.p.h., and (reverse) 3 m.p.h.

Regular steel wheels, skeleton steel wheels, and wheels with low-pressure tires are all available upon order. There is, of course, a wide variety of lugs, guide bands and extension rims.

More Work at Lower Cost

The Model "G" will especially appeal to the large-acreage corn grower because of its ability to handle a three-bottom plow, large disk harrow, four-row cultivator, two-row mounted corn picker, and to provide ample and steady belt power for threshing, grinding feed, pumping, and similar jobs.

The large-acreage cotton grower will appreciate it because of its ability to handle three-row bedders under all conditions, and four-row bedders under many conditions, four-row planters and cultivators.

The grain grower who also raises some corn or cotton will like it because it will handle row-crop work in addition to all the jobs necessary to the growing of small grains.

See the New John Deere Model "G" General Purpose Tractor at your dealer's store. Arrange for a field demonstration. Increase your yearly profit by cutting operating costs from plowing and planting time right on to the end of the harvest season.

Get the Feel of the Wheel...Ask Your Dealer for a Demonstration

A sales brochure for the Model G tractors.

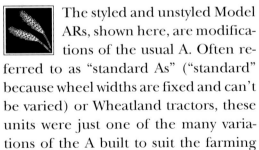 The styled and unstyled Model ARs, shown here, are modifications of the usual A. Often referred to as "standard As" ("standard" because wheel widths are fixed and can't be varied) or Wheatland tractors, these units were just one of the many variations of the A built to suit the farming conditions of a particular region, in this case the Midwest. The later model styled unit shown here **(above)** displays the low center of gravity, rear fenders, and heavy front axle characteristic of these tractors, while the unstyled tractor **(right)** retains the boxy component, or unintegrated appearance, of pre-1939 Deere tractors.

Early Model Bs were manufactured with what has come to be known as a four-bolt front end. Failure in the field resulted in a factory redesign, incorporating eight bolts to better handle the strain of daily toil.

The single-front-wheel model with the four-bolt pedestal is of particular interest. All early four-bolt Model Bs were officially referred to by the factory as "Garden Tractors," maybe not the best description given the fact Deere was trying to sell real tractors to real farmers. The unit shown here is serial number 1043 and is, in fact, the very first of only twenty-four tractors built with the single-wheel, four-bolt, Garden Tractor configuration. It was originally shipped to Phoenix, Arizona, in October of 1934, where it was eventually located by Lloyd Bellin and added to his and son Mike's collection.

This rusted unit has the closely spaced dual front wheels typically found on these tractors.

The New, MORE POWERFUL
JOHN DEERE Model "LA"

with all the
BALANCED FEATURES
of the
MODEL "L"

John Deere's latest contribution to better, faster, easier, more economical work on small-acreage farms.

THE success of the John Deere Model "L" Tractor on all types of small farms and as supplementary power on large farms has created a demand for the same efficient type of John Deere Tractor in a larger power size. John Deere engineers have produced such a tractor—the new Model "LA", shown above.

Built along the same general lines as the Model "L", the Model "LA" delivers about 45 per cent more power on belt and drawbar. It is about 500 pounds heavier than the Model "L", to provide balanced traction for the greater power. It handles all operations in growing and harvesting all crops, doing as much work in a day as four good work horses.

Now, two general purpose, standard tread tractors for small farms.

"L" "LA"

★ CHOOSE THE POWER SIZE THAT BEST FITS YOUR NEEDS ★

A brochure for Model LA tractors, declaring this "John Deere's latest contribution to better, faster, easier, more economical work on small-acreage farms."

Facing page: By 1947 another need had developed for a new addition to the Deere line. A unit produced by Ford-Ferguson was making serious inroads in the small tractor market and the Model L/LA Deere unit wasn't able to fend off this competitor. Utilizing Deere's first vertical two-cylinder engine (the L/LA series used Novo and then Hercules engines), the M model debuted in 1947. It incorporated a 20-horsepower engine and was a standard (nonadjustable wheel width) tractor with a PTO and electric starting as standard equipment. A host of more than twenty implements were released for use with this tractor, all designed around Deere's new Quik-Tatch hitching system. **Below:** The throttle control on an LA.

VERSATILITY
AND
HI-CROP TRACTORS

Pages 54–57: Hi-Crop tractors are always crowd-pleasers and attention-getters at today's threshing shows. These units again display the versatility inherent in Deere designs that allowed customization to suit specific needs. Used primarily for sugar cane farming in the southern United States, these tractors today are prize collector pieces offering a fascinating perspective on John Deere machinery. Shown on pages 54–55 **(large photo)** is a later Model AH (Hi-Crop)—note the pressed steel frame **(small photo)**. Also shown is a 720H manufactured between 1956 and 1958 **(above)**. Six-foot-tall Mike Bellin poses with his 1959 730 diesel **(left)** to provide perspective regarding the physical size of this unit. Only 120 examples of Bellin's unit were produced, with forty shipped out of the country. It's interesting to note that while Deere ceased two-cylinder tractor production in the United States in 1960, this particular model, two-cylinder engine and all, was produced in Argentina through 1970.

THE 4-PLOW "620" AND 5-PLOW "720" Hi-Crops
. . . ANSWER TO YOUR BIG-POWER NEEDS

GASOLINE OR ALL-FUEL ENGINES

The "620" and "720" Hi-Crop Tractors are regularly furnished with gasoline or all-fuel engines. These economical engines feature such "exclusives" as Duplex Carburetion and All-Weather Manifold.

If your requirements call for more power, your best tractor investment is a John Deere "620" or "720" Hi-Crop. These tractors offer big lugging power to handle large equipment at maximum working speed in tough conditions. Here's power that gives you more on-the-job help to make every job easier, get it done faster.

Special design all the way through assures top-quality work in tall, bushy crops. There's more than 32 inches of crop-saving clearance at every point under the tractor, 48 inches between final drive housings, plus a wide range of tread adjustability—60 to 84 inches front; 60 to 90 inches rear—adaptability which makes these "high steppers" ideally suited to your crop requirements.

When it comes to saving time on every job . . . to doing all jobs and doing them easier . . . to increasing quality of the work, these modern John Deere features are tops. *Custom* Powr-Trol offers you up to three separate hydraulic circuits for controlling all types of equipment—integral, drawn, or 3-point . . . instantly, accurately, and effortlessly with a finger-tip touch. *Independent* Power Take-Off delivers full engine power to speed jobs to completion, save costs and service upkeep of auxiliary engines. *Advanced* Power Steering takes the effort out of steering, leaves one hand free for operating controls. *Float-Ride* Seat absorbs the bumps, provides cushioned riding comfort. All the features that pay off in better work with greater operator comfort and convenience are yours.

Real dollars-and-cents savings are realized through greater fuel savings . . . minimum maintenance costs . . . and dependability and durability for year-after-year economy. Added to this is the big capacity of the "620" or "720" Hi-Crop and full line of equipment that lets you handle *more* jobs with a *single* tractor—slashing production costs. See your John Deere dealer soon and start farming the more profitable way with modern John Deere Tractor Power.

THE "720" DIESEL HI-CROP

All the performance and modern features of the regular "720," plus outstanding John Deere *Diesel* fuel economy, are yours with the John Deere "720" Hi-Crop *Diesel*. Here's the tractor that turns more fuel dollars into profit dollars . . . slashes operating costs with its hustling 5-plow power . . . and holds maintenance costs at rock-bottom. See your John Deere dealer and learn about all the many advantages that the "720" *Diesel* Hi-Crop offers you in fuel economy, big-work capacity, and modern features.

"620" AND "720" LP-GAS MODELS

From the ground up, John Deere LP-Gas Hi-Crop Tractors are *factory-engineered* to handle LP-fuels with maximum efficiency and economy. Both the "620" and "720" offer many special LP-Gas features including Duplex Carburetor, heavy-duty crankshaft, ignition with resistor bypass for easier starting . . . electric fuel shutoff . . . exhaust valve inserts and rotators . . . cool intake manifold . . . efficient fuel converter . . . and a completely sealed fuel system. Many of your LP-Gas questions are answered in the booklet, "John Deere LP-Gas Tractors." See your John Deere dealer or write John Deere, Moline, Ill., for your free copy.

11

A sales brochure for 420, 620, and 720 Hi-Crop tractors and equipment.

Both photos: Ok, so what do you think it is? It's obviously a styled, later edition Model B (note the pressed steel frame) and it's clearly configured as a Hi-Crop. It has what appears to be John Deere part numbers all over it (or are they really from an after-market supplier who wanted to have its parts appear to be factory?), and it has a narrow front. Wouldn't it be called a BNH (Hi-Crop)? The only problem is that while some styled BNHs are shown in the Deere record books as having been built through 1940, the term "Hi-Crop" in 1940 did not mean the pedestal extension and dropped rear wheel gear cases seen on this unit. Hi-Crop simply meant slightly larger rear wheels similar to other early Hi-Crop units noted elsewhere in this book. Whatever the case, restorer Mike Bellin has never seen another unit like it, nor has he seen pictures of any similar units in his travels or talked with other restorers who can positively identify the tractor. Possibly it's a factory experimental unit that somehow got into private hands, or it might be a B modified with after-market parts. Whatever the case, it appears to be a unique, possibly one-of-a-kind John Deere. One thing for sure, a Model B sitting this high off the ground sure catches your attention.

50 shown here **(top inset)** is a 1955 or 1956 row crop unit with adjustable rear wheels and a single front wheel. The Model 70 **(large photo)** is another row crop tricycle with closely spaced front wheels and was manufactured between 1953 and 1956. The 620 **(bottom inset)** was produced between 1956 and 1958. Shown below is a detail of an LP-powered unit.

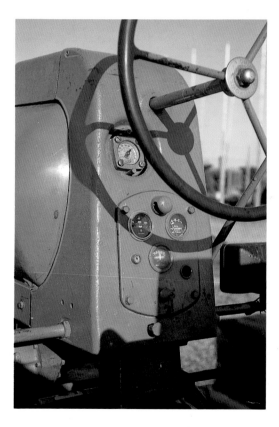

 Like other manufacturers, Deere produced limited quantities of LP gas-fueled tractors. Demand for these units tended to be regional in nature, especially where market conditions and proximity to refinery facilities made lower energy propane fuel competitive with or even advantageous over standard fuels. The Model

DIESELS, CRAWLERS, AND NON-TRACTOR EQUIPMENT

 The year 1949 marked another breakthrough for John Deere with the introduction of its first diesel-powered unit. The culmination of research and testing over nearly thirteen years, including the production of sixteen prototype units and 66,000 hours of field testing, resulted in the new Model R **(page 63, small photo),** which was an early success in the field. Nebraska Tractor Test number 406, conducted during April of 1949, recorded a bare weight of 7,603 pounds, 51 brake horsepower, and 45.7 drawbar horsepower. With a 5.75-inch bore and eight-inch stroke, the massive two-cylinder engine displaced 416 cubic inches.

In 1955 an upgraded heavyweight diesel was introduced: the Model 80 **(page 62–63, large photo).** With bore enlarged to 6 1/8-inch and stroke remaining the same at eight inches, the new two-cylinder engine now displaced 471.5 cubic inches and produced 67.6 brake and 61.8 drawbar horsepower and 422.6 foot-pounds of torque.

By 1958 Deere had upgraded the Model 80 to the Model 830 **(above left),** with a belt output of 75 horsepower and a drawbar output of 69.6 horsepower. Designed as a six-plow machine, this unit could be ordered with either a four-cylinder gas starting motor or a new electric cranking motor.

THE *NEW* JOHN DEERE

MODEL *80* *DIESEL*

BRINGS YOU BIG CAPACITY AT ROCK-BOTTOM OPERATING COSTS

IT'S *ANOTHER*
JOHN DEERE
POWER STEERING
TRACTOR

The Model "80" Diesel is a powerful new John Deere Tractor with the brawn to plow a *six-foot* strip . . . to handle *twenty-one feet* of double-action disk harrow . . . to pull *double* hookups of hydraulically controlled field cultivators, tool carriers, rod weeders, grain drills. Here's capacity that will greatly increase your daily work output—that may even save you the cost of a second tractor and driver.

Along with its big capacity, the new Model "80" offers you amazing economy on *both* fuel and maintenance. In factory fuel-economy tests, it measured up in every way to the championship performance records

set by other John Deere Diesel Tractors tested at Lincoln, Nebraska. Its simple, rugged two-cylinder design and its high-quality construction insure years of low-cost service.

So read the inside pages for the facts about this great new tractor. Then see it at your John Deere dealer's, and arrange for a field demonstration. You'll agree it's the extra-quality tractor in the 5-plow field—the tractor that will cut costs on large-scale farming operations.

This brochure boasted about the new Model 80 Diesel, *"another* John Deere *power steering* tractor."

 Above: The year 1952 marked the end of the Model A. Deere replaced the A with the Model 60 and the B with the Model 50, beginning an era of number, rather than letter, model designations. The new Model 60 incorporated a number of changes including, for the first time, a water pump in the cooling system, a two-barrel carburetor, a hot and cold intake manifold for faster warm-ups, and a quick-change rear tread provision. Shown here is a standard (nonadjustable wheel tread) or Wheatland version of the Model 60 with its heavy cast iron front axle. **Right:** In order from left to right is a 1956 John Deere 80, a 1956 820, and a 1959 830. All await their day of restoration. The 830 marked the end of the John Deere two-cylinder diesel engine, and was phased out in 1960.

They're Newcomers with a Pedigree

MEET THE John Deere "50" and "60" Tractors—the brilliant new successors to the famous John Deere Models "B" and "A."

These heavy-duty, two- and three-plow tractors offer you many new operating advantages that will save time and speed up every power job on your farm . . . that will save work and make your farming easier than ever before . . . that will greatly increase the operating efficiency of your equipment and boost profits.

The Models "50" and "60" are newcomers with a pedigree of almost thirty years' experience in building more than a million farm tractors. In addition to their many new engineering advancements and major improvements shown on the following pages, they offer you all the time-tested, field-proved advantages of exclusive John Deere *two-cylinder* engine design. They're blue-ribbon, quality-built tractors through and through.

THE HEAVY-DUTY 2-PLOW **50**

THE HEAVY-DUTY 3-PLOW **60**

...*featuring* Duplex Carburetion . . . "Live" Power Shaft . . . "Live," High-Pressure Hydraulic Powr-Trol . . . Quick-Change Wheel-Tread . . . Effortless Steering, and many other <u>new</u> features and major engineering improvements

(3)

A sales brochure for Models 50 and 60.

 Pages 69–71: As was the case with most agricultural equipment manufacturers in search of other ways to sell their equipment, John Deere produced both industrial and commercial versions of their units. When it came to crawlers, Deere established a joint venture with the Lindeman Power Equipment Company in Yakima, Washington, wherein Lindeman would modify Deere tractors by manufacturing and installing crawler tracks and drive assemblies. Beginning in 1939, approximately 1,600 units, based on the Model B, were manufactured and relabled Model BO—the O standing for orchard use, the primary application for these units **(left).**

By 1946 Deere was making plans to phase out the Model B tractor, and so advised the Lindeman organization, at the same time inquiring about their interest in continuing crawler production based on the forthcoming Model M tractor **(page 70–71, large photo)** with the new vertical two-cylinder engine. Agreement was reached to continue production based on this new unit, an agreement which soon thereafter resulted in purchase of the Lindeman operation by John Deere & Company in January of 1947.

In 1953 the M series, in keeping with the number rather than letter model des-

ignations, evolved into the 40 series. The 40 was a light-to-medium-duty unit in line with its Model M heritage and embodied the usual Deere versatility with standard row crop and wide front options.

In 1956 Deere introduced the 420 **(above).** Advertising from the period shows ten versions of this tractor available from the factory including two crawlers, a Hi-Crop, and a single-front-wheel unit. Not displayed in the farm-oriented advertisement is the industrial version, captured here at a threshing show in Le Sueur, Minnesota, home of the Jolly Green Giant (the Green Giant vegetable canning company).

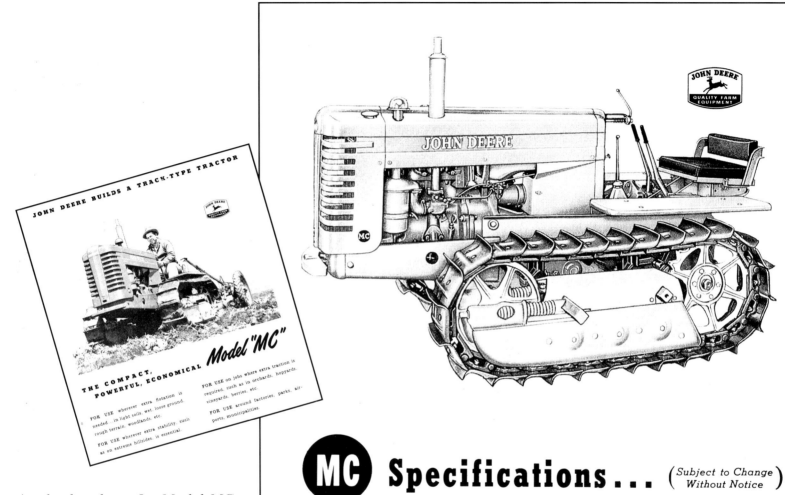

A sales brochure for Model MC tractors.

MC Specifications... $\left(\begin{array}{c}\textit{Subject to Change}\\ \textit{Without Notice}\end{array}\right)$

CAPACITY—2-3-plow; 8-foot double-action disk harrow and similar loads

SPEEDS
First   —1.2 M.P.H.
Second —2.2 M.P.H.
Third   —2.9 M.P.H.
Fourth —6.0 M.P.H.
Reverse—1.0 M.P.H.

BELT PULLEY—Extra Equipment
Diameter—7-1/4"
Face—6"
Revolutions per minute—1575
Belt Speed (feet per minute)—3100

POWER TAKE-OFF—Regular equipment
Revolutions per minute—550

(Continued on next page)

Both photos: Recall for a moment that in the beginning, Deere was a plow manufacturer who progressed to the production of a variety of tilling, cultivating, and related agricultural products. One of the more important reasons Deere subsequently entered the tractor business was the hope that selling tractors would result in selling more of their principle products—plows, cultivators, and the like. The hoped-for result of that strategy is shown here: a vintage one-row John Deere corn picker mounted on a 1939 John Deere Model A. Note the radiator screen designed to keep residue away from the radiator and prevent overheating.

LOADER
REAR MOUNTED
BUILT 1939-1940

Both photos: Another piece of interesting Deere factory equipment is represented by this rear-mounted, cable-actuated loader restored by Gerald Schmidt from Hinckley, Minnesota. This unit is displayed mounted on a Model A. Its primary use was to load manure wagons. This design was produced in 1939 and 1940 before being abandoned in favor of more conventional front-mounted units.

Above: Maintaining a separator in proper working condition when it's brand new is a challenge. Making one operate properly when it is fifty to sixty years old is another story. Here we see a Deere unit shut down for adjustment or repair during a weekend threshing show in the Midwest. While Deere had a strong beginning in nontractor farm equipment, and companies such as Case had been manufacturing threshing equipment and separators since the 1860s, it was not until 1929 that Deere first became involved with separators when it purchased the failing Wagner-Langemo Company of Minneapolis, Minnesota. **Left:** A John Deere single-bottom plow. Note the tractor wheel weights.

Above: With acquisition of the Waterloo Gasoline Engine Company in 1918, primarily for the tractor line, Deere was immediately in the small stationary engine business. During the 1920s Deere & Company released a new line of engines in the 1.5 to 6 horsepower range, which highlighted a fully enclosed crankcase, a feature not at all common during the period. Of the units seen here, one is powering a corn sheller, just one of the many uses that farm families found for these units.

A John Deere

Gasoline

Engine . . . .

Saves Time

Saves Money

Saves Muscle

YOUR time is valuable. Today, more than ever before, it is necessary to save time and labor on the farm. That is why so many farmers are turning to the John Deere gasoline engine to pump water, shell corn, run the grindstone, saw wood, grind feed, and do other "odd-jobs." It is also the reason why so many farm women are using it for churning, separating cream, and running the washing machine.

From morning till night, day in and day out, this handy "chore boy" works its way into the favor of everyone in the family. It is a time-saver for mother, father, son, and daughter.

BECAUSE the John Deere gasoline engine is precision-built, it is a money-saver. All vital parts are completely enclosed and kept dust and dirt free. Automatic oiling, simplicity of construction and ease of adjustment add years to its working life. These are only a few of the many reasons why operating and upkeep costs are exceptionally low; why the John Deere engine will save money for you throughout its long life.

THERE'S no longer any need for doing many slow, tedious farm jobs by hand. Save hard work by using a John Deere gasoline engine. It acts as a faithful servant in lightening the labor-load of the entire family. Even in starting, it is a muscle-saver. The proper gas-air mixture plus a hot, fat spark makes starting both quick and easy.

3

JOHN DEERE
GASOLINE
ENGINES

When you buy John Deere Implements you are sure of prompt repair service during their long life.

A sales brochure for John Deere gasoline engines.

Left top: Tractor fuels were a constant area of controversy and concern from the earliest days through the 1940s and 1950s. Refining techniques and product qualities were not at all standardized in early days. Additionally, tractors were often designed to be started and warmed up on one type of fuel—gasoline—and then operated under load on a second type of fuel—kerosene. Refineries also produced a witches' brew loosely described by the name "distillate" or "tractor distillate," which didn't really tell the purchaser anything significant about its formulation for tractor use.

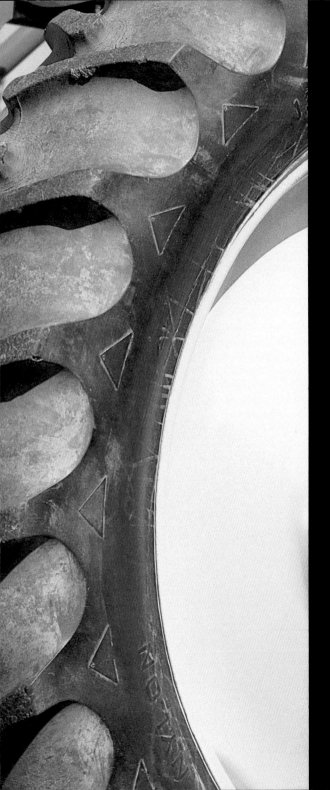

CLOSE-UPS
AND
RARE TRACTORS

JOHN DEERE
CUSTOM
POWR - TROL

Pages 80–81, large photo: For the vast number of early Model A and B owners, hand-starting their tractors was a daily fact of life. Knowing where a piston was located within a cylinder was important to minimize the effort necessary to get the engine firing. Flywheels came with notations cast in the surface. The owner of this styled Model A, as a part of his restoration, has highlighted this information. **Small photo:** From its earliest days, Deere was know for its power assist devices.

 Right and below: Magnetos were the only ignition on early John Deere tractors, and manufacturers such as Fairbanks Morse, Dixie, Wico, Edison-Splitdorf, and others vied for the right to fire the two-cylinder Deere engines of the period. Hand-starting meant relatively slow revolution of the engine during start up, a condition under which a magneto generates almost no current with which to fire a spark plug. As a result, all magnetos on Deere tractors were equipped with an impulse coupling, an internal mechanism that made the magneto spin faster during a part of its revolution, thus generating enough current. Once the engine was running at idle speed or faster, the magneto would then be operating at a high enough RPM to generate adequate current without the aid of the impulse coupling.

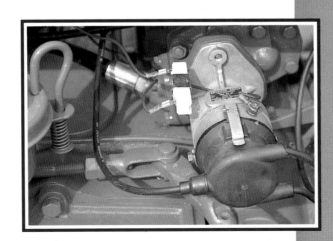

Properly hand-starting a Deere two-cylinder engine was dependent on a compression release seen here as the bronze-colored piece mounted alongside the spark plug. Opening these small orifices, one on each cylinder, allowed enough compression to escape so that the engine could be turned over by hand. With any luck, the engine would fire and begin to run, with very loudly hissing jets of combustion gasses escaping from the open releases. Rotating the handle on the compression releases closed the openings, shut off the escaping gasses, and settled the engine down to the steady irregular idle characteristic of only the two-cylinder John Deere engine.

Left: Highlighted in this close-up of a Model G engine is an ignition wire guard that conducts and protects the plug wire from near its source under the hood to the plug. Given the general use of farm equipment and the less-than-protected location of spark plugs and ignition wires on Deere horizontal two-cylinder engines, it's interesting to wonder why guards of this nature were not mounted on the earliest units manufactured by the company. **Below:** Earlier Deere flat-head engine designs carried spark plugs in a more protected location.

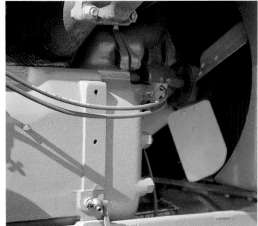

TO TIGHTEN CLUTCH-SET LEVER IN RUNNING
POSITION, TIGHTEN EACH NUT ONE SLOT TO RIGHT,
REPLACE COTTERS. REPEAT IF NECESSARY
READ INSTRUCTION BOOK.

Dir. No. 6-Tractor   Printed in U.S.A.

Facing page: Simplicity and ease of maintenance were two guiding principles by which Deere designed and manufactured tractors. Competitors' conventional mounting of engines and drivelines, similar to that of a typical automobile, could never provide the ease of accessibility to the clutch for routine maintenance and adjustment found on John Deere tractors. Considering the heavy use a tractor clutch receives and the materials and design technologies of the 1920s and 1930s, having the clutch mechanism mounted in such an easily accessible location as found on Deere tractors was an important maintenance advantage as well as a strong selling feature.

Right and pages 88–89: Farmers of the 1920s and 1930s, making a transition from animal to mechanical horsepower, often had a very poor understanding of what they were getting into. Overwork a farm animal a little, give it a few extra days rest, and often as not it was ok. Abuse a piece of mechanical equipment and the

damage would be permanent, if not fatal, to the engine or transmission. Lubricant levels, clean fuel, proper greasings, clean filters: All were critical to the longevity of tractors of the period. Manufacturers learned early on that failure of a mishandled piece of farm equipment was never the operator's fault. The blame always fell on the manufacturer as the builder of a poor piece of equipment—an opinion that would be voiced loud and often at the feed mill, town meeting, or church social.

One way in which companies such as Deere dealt with this problem was to put decals anywhere and everywhere on their equipment to educate and remind the operator of his responsibility. Note especially the large decal on the fuel tank of the Model D (**facing page**), which details engine lubrication procedures. The reason tractors of this vintage had two drain cocks on the oil sump is related to the poor quality of fuels commonly used in farm tractors and the limited sealing capabilities of piston rings of the period. Fuels of the day often burned poorly and incompletely. Piston rings simply didn't seal well against cylinder walls. The result was that engine oil sumps often accumulated significant quantities of unburned fuel, which caused many prob-

lems including overfilling the sump. This resulted in aeration of the oil as the crankshaft and connecting rod splashed through the now-diluted lubricant. This caused air bubbles in the pressurized oil lines and ultimately bearing failure as diluted and aerated oil reached critical areas under heavy load. Checking the upper drain cock ensured that the lubricant didn't exceed that level and that the sump wasn't overfilled and subject to aeration.

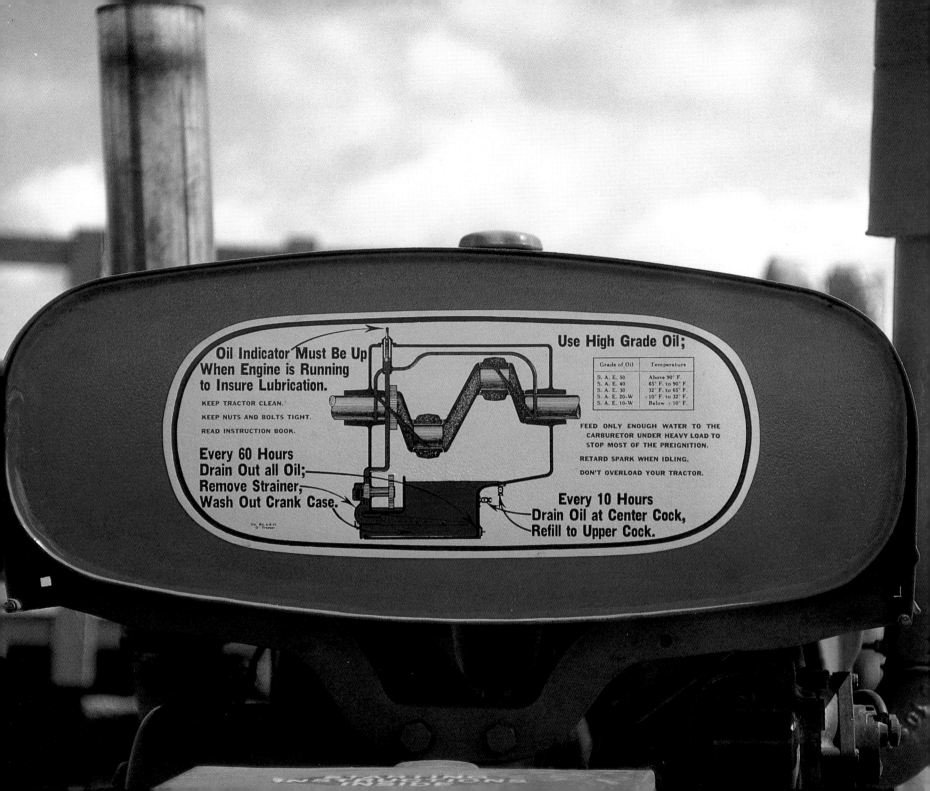

Pages 90–91: Pictured here is a rare unit produced by John Deere in 1939. Designated a BWH40, there were approximately twelve of these units manufactured, with fewer than five accounted for today. The figure 40 in the model designation denotes the very narrow forty-inch width to which wheel tread could be reduced for vegetable farming. Note that front and rear axle housings had to be shortened in order to accommodate the forty-inch width and that the tractor is offset to the left on its wheelbase **(below).** This unit is part of a fine collection of rare and unique John Deere equipment acquired and restored by the father and son team of Lloyd and Mike Bellin from Isanti, Minnesota.

 All photos: A 1935 Model BW. Versatility was a key element in the Deere design philosophy, and the Model BW demonstrated that concept. The tread on Mike Bellin's unstyled 1935 Model BW (Wide) can be adjusted in front and back from a narrow fifty-six inches to a maximum width of eighty inches. With only a one-plow capacity and maximum flexibility, this unit was designed by Deere to be used extensively for cultivation purposes.

Facing page and below: If Darth Vader (or in the case of the older generation, Buck Rogers) were to design his own custom John Deere tractor, it would just have to look like this unit—a 1952 AO. The designation O, of course, signifying an Orchard model, makes this is a Model A modified for use in orchards. The object of the streamlined sheet metal is to allow the operator to work as closely as possible around fruit trees without damaging low-hanging branches. While it is the sheet metal that makes these tractors unique and interesting, it is that same sheet metal that makes restoration extra difficult. Restorer Mike Bellin reports that the fenders and cowl sections on this unit were heavily battered and damaged, requiring far more than the normal mechanical work necessary to restore most tractors.

John Deere Model "AO" Streamlined Grove and Orchard Tractor

One glance at this new John Deere Model "AO" Grove and Orchard Tractor and you know that it is a tractor specially designed for grove, orchard, vineyard, and hopyard.

Notice the fully-streamlined, low-down design . . . the narrow, compact construction . . . the short wheel base . . . the full enclosure of chassis, rear wheels, belt pulley, and flywheel . . . not a thing to catch branches, to injure blossoms, to bruise fruit. A real orchard tractor.

And under those smooth, flowing lines is John Deere Economy. Simplicity. Dependability . . . fewer, more rugged parts that last longer . . . easier maintenance . . . straight-line transmission with no bevel gears to consume power. In addition, there is the ability to burn the low-cost fuels efficiently and successfully.

There are four practical speeds, too—2, 3, 4, and 6-1 4 miles an hour . . . a large, comfortable seat . . . compact platform . . . built-in power shaft . . . independently operated differential brakes that make for short turns at the end of the tree rows . . . power to handle the load ordinarily pulled by a six-horse team.

Get the feel of this new Streamlined Model "AO" out in the grove or orchard. Notice how easily it handles . . . the convenience of all controls . . . the perfect view of the work . . . the comfort of the dust-proof, full skirted fenders . . . the easily adjusted hitch. Not a thing has been overlooked.

You've never seen a finer orchard tractor. Shown here with special citrus fenders which are an extra.

The sales brochure for the Model AO. The caption for the photograph reads, "You've never seen a finer orchard tractor. Shown here with special citrus fenders which are an extra."

Left: There are Hi-Crop tractors and then there are Hi-Crop tractors. Both of the large units in this photo are Hi-Crops. The unstyled tractor is a 1938 ANH, and only twenty-six were built. It ran on forty-inch rear wheels, and in 1938 that made this Model A with a single front a Narrow (N) Hi-Crop (H). Note the extensive rear wheel spline for width adjustment. The unit alongside is a 1959 630 Hi-Crop, of which only sixteen were constructed. Ground clearance is by now significantly increased over the 1938 unit by virtue of dropped rear wheel cases and extended front axle uprights, which greatly increased ground clearance for Southern sugar cane farmers. At the other extreme from the Hi-Crop tractors is the obviously "low crop" Model L, dwarfed by its big brothers.

Left: From its earliest days with the acquisition of the Waterloo Engine Works and the subsequent production of small John Deere stationary engines, portable power units were a part of the Deere product line. With the development of a reliable, proven tractor engine, it was only logical that Deere enter the large stationary engine market with a product of its own. Used for logging, sawmill work, and a wide range of other applications, these units were simple adaptations of a proven product. Shown here is a 1946 type W-III. Note the small gasoline tank at the end of the hood with a second fuel cap on top, indicating a multifuel capability. As with normal tractor engines, this unit was capable of being started and warmed up on gasoline (small tank) and then operated under load on a less expensive fuel such as kerosene or other distillate fuels.

Facing page: This tricycle is a Hi-Crop tractor—specifically a BNH, meaning a Model B, Narrow front, Hi-Crop—and was built in 1938. It too carried forty-inch rear wheels, raising it high enough off the ground to be classified as a Hi-Crop in its day. Of particular interest regarding this unit is the extremes to which rear wheels can be adjusted to accommodate a wide range of row crops. With the rear wheels moved inward as far as possible, the minimum width is a relatively slim fifty-six inches. With the rear wheels moved outward as far as possible on the axle shafts, the width becomes eighty inches, and with the rear wheels reversed, taking advantage of the offset center hubs, the maximum width between rear wheels becomes 104 inches.

Left: Every vintage tractor enthusiast, at least every John Deere enthusiast, should have a yard ornament like this! The unstyled B with plow oversees the prairie landscape at the Lloyd Bellin residence in Isanti, Minnesota. **Overleaf:** The year 1960 saw the end of the two-cylinder era at Deere & Company and with it the introduction of new equipment providing an ever-decreasing farm population with the tools to work ever-larger farms. Scenes such as this became commonplace as benefits of the agricultural revolution, begun by pioneers such as John Deere, reached full bloom. *(Photo copyright © by Dick Dietrich)*

AWAITING
RESTORATION

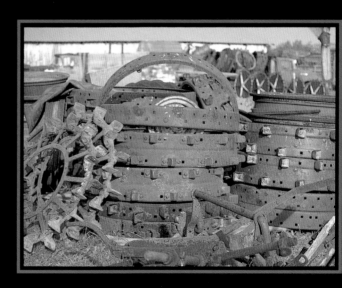

 Pages 104–105, large photo: A 1947 Model B, purchased brand new by Lloyd Bellin's grandfather and still owned by the family, sits nearly fifty years later, awaiting the day when it too will be returned to better-than-new condition. **Small photo:** A ready supply of rear steel wheels for various tractors awaits restorers. Note the less common skeletal wheels to the left, so called for obvious reasons, and the additional truck load of wheels in the background.

Left and below: Awash in a sea of prairie grasses on the Libis farm in Eureka, South Dakota, this late Model B appears to have been at work in relatively recent times.

 Pages 108–110: Boneyards, scrap yards—whatever you call them, backlots that are often the temporary resting place for old tractors are an endless source of fascination and parts for the restorer. It is in these lots that the rare and obscure often are located, having been left there because of a mechanical problem for which their uniqueness made repairs at the time seem improbable or uneconomical. Here we see a Model A **(large photo)** from which many parts have been taken, a Model B **(top inset)** missing rear tires and rims, and a Model GP **(bottom inset)** and a Model L **(overleaf)** missing a great deal. All likely donated their parts to shiny restored units participating somewhere in a threshing show.

INDEX

For enthusiasts interested in a clubs and publications dedicated to John Deere tractors, call or write:

Two-Cylinder Club
308 East G Avenue
Grundy Center, Iowa 50638
(319) 824-5487

Green Magazine
Richard Hain, Editor
RR 1
Bee, Nebraska 68314